Faithbuilders Bible Studies

The Second Epistle of Saint Peter

by Mathew Bartlett & Derek Williams

WIPF & STOCK · Eugene, Oregon

Wipf and Stock Publishers
199 W 8th Ave, Suite 3
Eugene, OR 97401

The Second Epistle of Saint Peter
By Bartlett, Mathew and Williams, Derek
Copyright©2019 Apostolos
ISBN 13: 978-1-5326-9606-0
Publication date 7/7/2019
Previously published by Apostolos, 2019

Dedicated to all those who are hungry for God's word.

More from Faithbuilders Bible Studies

Faithbuilders Bible Studies

The Faithbuilders Bible study series has been developed as a useful resource for today's students of God's word and their busy lifestyles. Pastors, home or study group leaders and indeed for anyone wishing to study the Bible for themselves will benefit from using Faithbuilders studies.

Each volume is the result of many years of group Bible study, and has been revised in order to be relevant, challenging and faith building whilst remaining clear and easy to understand, helping more people to discover the blessings of God's word.

Mathew Bartlett has been a church minister for almost 30 years. He holds a master's degree in Biblical Studies from the University of Chester, England. Derek Williams is a retired pastor and preacher with over 40 years of experience.

Contents

Introduction, Authorship and Date

Author, Date and Place of Writing

The author of this letter identifies himself as the Simeon Peter, an apostle (1:1). Simeon (Simon) was the fisherman from Galilee whom Jesus called to be his disciple and surnamed "Peter," "the rock." It is generally believed that he was writing around AD 65, and certainly before AD 68 (Nero's death), because tradition has it that Peter was executed by order of Nero. Little is known about the place of the letter's composition, though the idea that he was writing from Rome is not far-fetched. The letter is addressed more generally than 1 Peter, to all who share the Christian faith. However, 3:1 implies that Peter is writing to the same audience in each letter.

Although the themes of the letter tend to confirm genuine Petrine authorship (for example, the author claims to be a witness of the Transfiguration in 1:16–18), many modern scholars find reason to believe it was written by someone else, perhaps a student of Peter. Among these arguments are the Hellenistic style of writing, the idea that by "false-teaching" the letter is referencing second-century Gnosticism, and the idea of Paul's letters being on a par with Scripture. Yet the letter was recognized as genuine from early times, and the fact that the author claims knowledge of the letters of Paul as current documents and implies a personal acquaintance with him ("our dear brother") may as much imply genuine Petrine authorship as deny it – especially since this would agree with the accounts of their meetings in both Acts and Galatians. Indeed, the inclusion of 3:15–16 may be thought of as an attempt to heal the rift between the two men.

Moreover, in terms of the style of Greek used, as was the case with 1 Peter, where the style may be explained by the note (5:12) that the apostle received help from Silas in writing the epistle, so the fact that 2 Peter contains rather Hellenised Greek could be explained in the same way, albeit in this case the amanuensis is not named. Likewise, those who claim the letter deals with Gnosticism fail to appreciate that Peter here does not offer any details of the false teaching under discussion – so it remains possible that a much earlier error may be in view. Also, it is possible that the appreciation of Paul's letters at least containing teaching which should be viewed on a par with Scripture is evident in early and genuine Pauline letters (see 1 Cor 14:37; 1 Thess 4:2). Therefore, I find attempts to deny Peter's authorship of this letter unconvincing.

Similarities to Jude

There are clear similarities between 2 Peter (particularly chapter 2) and Jude. Several theories have been put forward to explain the similarities (for example, did Peter redact Jude? Did Jude quote Peter? Did both Jude and Peter quote another document which we no longer have access to?). However, these issues will not be discussed in this study. Although I personally regard Jude borrowing from Peter as the most convincing scenario, it is vital to realize that none of the theories have any great impact on our understanding and application of the text.

Purpose of Letter

The Second Epistle of Peter has several key purposes. It contains clear statements of major Christian doctrines, such as the infallibility of Scripture, the fulfillment of God's promises in Christ, the "now but not yet" aspect of the believer's inheritance in Christ, and the reality of the believer's eternal hope, focussed on Christ's near return which will usher in the promise of a new heaven and a new earth.

Notably, 2 Peter also contains dire warnings against following the lifestyle and pattern of teaching adopted by "false teachers." Although Peter (in common with Jude) tells us very little about what these people were actually teaching, he discusses their vices (and coming judgment) at length, so that the early church might learn to avoid all such behaviors.

The apparent delay in the return of Christ is the subject of chapter 3, and interestingly it is not dealt with in terms that turn attention away from the Parousia and instead focus on mission here and now. Rather, it explains that God's timetable is not the same as the human timetable. Christ will come, and this is certain, for no matter how long it may take, the promise will be kept. Indeed, "a single day is like a thousand years with the Lord and a thousand years are like a single day" (3:8). Not only that, but Peter also offers a reason for the apparent delay, in terms of God's patience with humanity, for God, "does not wish for any to perish but for all to come to repentance." (3:9).

2 Peter 1

Themes in Chapter 1

In this second general letter, Peter reveals his concern that the early Christian church should become a cohesive community characterized by its diligent obedience to Christ, and veneration of holy Scripture; a community which treasures all the scriptural promises of God which have now found their fulfillment in Jesus Christ. As a result, the community would experience the transforming power of the Scriptures, and thus be recognized by all as a community transformed by God's grace, displaying godly virtues, which in itself would be a testimony to the validity of the gospel.

The Scriptures give us a clear understanding of who God is and of what he has achieved for us through Christ's death and resurrection. As believers we have been born again to eternal life through this incorruptible message from God, and by the same figure our growth in the life of godliness is also made possible through our response of faith to God's word.

In Peter's view, although the blessings of our sharing Christ's nature are ours now, yet we still await the fuller manifestation of these blessings which will be brought about by Christ when he returns. This theme has been carried forward from Peter's first epistle, where salvation was to be revealed "in the last time" (1 Peter 1:5). It is a subject to which Peter will return briefly in chapter 2 (in 2:9 he speaks of the day of judgment) and more fully in chapter 3 (especially 3:3–13), so it must be of great importance to him and has great relevance today. The appearance of Christ will be the culmination of all God's purposes for his people.

While we wait for this eschatological perfection, Peter reminds us that we have already become God's children by faith in Christ, and that as God's children we can – in the present time – grow to spiritual maturity in our knowledge of him, and in our likeness to him. This growth in Christ is achieved by the Holy Spirit through his influencing our heartfelt obedience to the revealed will of God contained in Scripture.

Growing in godliness may be a difficult process, but it also brings many benefits. Growing in faith, virtue, knowledge, self-control, perseverance, godliness, brotherly love and affection will help us live better lives now; but it is also a necessary part of God's preparing us for eternal life. Moreover, it will result in blessing for others who come into contact with God's nature of love, patience and grace only as they witness these qualities in his children.

Peter knew that he would soon die, for Jesus had predicted this following his resurrection (1:13–15). Yet his confidence is clear. His hope for eternal life, like ours, is based on the fact that what God has foretold in the Scriptures he had now fulfilled in Christ. Peter was privileged to be someone who had witnessed Christ's glory in the transfiguration, and later became a witness of Christ death and resurrection. Death held no terrors for him, for he had already seen the glory which awaited him beyond life. It is likely that Peter shared his personal confidence in eternal life as an example for the believers. As the church held diligently to the confirmed truth it possessed, it would have no fear of future events, or of death itself.

Verse-by-Verse

Greetings

1:1 From Simeon Peter, a slave and apostle of Jesus Christ, to those who through the righteousness of our God and Savior, Jesus Christ, have been granted a faith just as precious as ours.

The author of the letter is Simeon (Simon) one of the fishermen from Galilee who were called by Christ to be among the original twelve apostles. Christ later surnamed him "Peter" ("the rock," see John 1:42) and despite Simon's early failures, this name may have been given as a prediction of his eventual unwavering commitment to the faith. Although Simon Peter could claim the office and title of an apostle in relation to the church, yet in relation to Jesus Christ he still considers himself to be merely a servant. The word translated "slave" in the NET above is better rendered "servant" since it carries the idea of free-will service. In fact, in Old Testament language, the servant of the Lord is an honored position. It is an honor for us to serve the Lord!

The letter is addressed to all who had the same precious faith that the apostles had. Since the second epistle is addressed to the same group of people as the first (2 Pet 3:1), it appears Peter may have intended both letters to be read by Christian generally.

For Peter, there is only one faith. As Ephesians 4:5 explains, both Jews and Gentiles alike share the same faith in Christ. This faith is "granted" because it is the gift of God (Eph 2:8). God gave his only begotten Son to die for our sins. He rose again to give us eternal life. This is the foundation of our Christian faith. Having judged sin on the cross, God is justly able to justify and pardon guilty sinners for their crimes "through the righteousness of our God" (see Rom 3:25–26).

1:2 May grace and peace be lavished on you as you grow in the rich knowledge of God and of Jesus our Lord!

What a wonderful greeting and desire from the apostle for his readers, that they might enjoy the grace, peace, and knowledge of God in their lives. The grace (unmerited favor of God) and perfect wholeness and heart peace which is ours through the Lord Jesus Christ will overflow in our lives as we grow in the full, personal, precise and correct knowledge of God and of Jesus our Lord. It should be our desire to see others blessed by these great spiritual blessings. As we seek the well-being of others, we can make this our constant prayer.

Growing in Grace and Godliness

1:3 I can pray this because his divine power has bestowed on us everything necessary for life and godliness through the rich knowledge of the one who called us by his own glory and excellence.

All that we need to live a godly life has been freely bestowed on us through God's divine power in action. The act of divine power in question is the Christ event (encompassing all aspects of Christ's life, death, resurrection and exaltation), and it is through this that God has made us his children (Jas 1:18). By this same action, God reveals his Son in us (2 Cor 3:18) and to us (2 Cor 4:6). God has called us to share his glory, which is the excellence of his own nature, so that he might change us into his likeness (Rom 8:29). Evidently, the process of our inner transformation to share God's nature will result in outer conformity to godly living, for godliness literally means "God-likeness" (Eph 5:1). The better we get to know God, the fuller our transformation will be.

1:4 Through these things he has bestowed on us his precious and most magnificent promises, so that by means of what was promised you may become partakers of the divine nature, after escaping the worldly corruption that is produced by evil desire.

God has revealed his Son to us through Scripture, and all that we receive from God comes as we respond to that revelation by faith. Peter has already said that we are made partakers of the divine nature by our having been born of God through the incorruptible seed of his word (see 1 Pet 1:23). Consequently, it is through the word of God that we receive all that we need to grow in the likeness of Christ. Clearly, God's word must be central in all aspects of our discipleship and ministry.

Since Christ died for our sin, our sinful nature is reckoned by God as having died with Him and we now share the eternal life of Christ. This is how we have escaped the corruption that is in the world. This works out in practice as we learn to say "no" to the old nature, and "yes" to the new. This is the way we "grow in godliness," as Peter unfolds in the next few verses. Paul concurs with Peter in Colossians 3:1–17, where he explains the idea of putting off the "old self" and following the "new self" in Christ.

1:5 For this very reason, make every effort to add to your faith excellence, to excellence, knowledge;

As well as giving us the theological or spiritual explanation of how believers in Christ share the divine nature, Peter also offers practical instructions on how we can develop Christ-likeness. On our part we must do our utmost to grow in Christ, using all the means God has given us. As we do, God will do his part, and lead us to grow in Christ; albeit at his pace, not ours. Just as a baby does not grow into an adult overnight, neither shall we mature in Christ all at once. Yet as we grow in Christ, certain Christ-like characteristics will develop and become evident in our lives.

We have already received saving faith as the gift of God, and as we exercise that faith in following Christ it will cause us to develop an excellent character (virtue), "the excellence of Christ's character" AMP. J. B. Phillips calls it, "Real goodness of life." We must also develop knowledge; that is, the knowledge of God, his will, and ways.

1:6–7 to knowledge, self-control; to self-control, perseverance; to perseverance, godliness; to godliness, brotherly affection; to brotherly affection, unselfish love.

As we come to recognize God's will, and are willing to obey it, so we become more self-controlled, habitually choosing to yield to God's will. This process leads us to develop perseverance in our Christian experience; that is, so that we will go on with the Lord despite the problems that come our way. Our perseverance will lead us to develop other Christ-like qualities, which are summed up in the word "godliness." To be like Christ means developing brotherly kindness, and that deep down genuine brotherly or sisterly love which is the summation of Christian character.

The result of this kind of spiritual growth in the church today will be exactly the same as it was in Peter's day – those who develop virtues such as brotherly love and the knowledge of God will not be riven by dissent or rivalry, but will present a united witness to the world outside the believing community.

1:8 For if these things are really yours and are continually increasing, they will keep you from becoming ineffective and unproductive in your pursuit of knowing our Lord Jesus Christ more intimately.

If these qualities are present and are continuing to grow in our lives, then we will have a beneficial effect on all around us. We will be living witnesses as others see Christ living in us. The result of our spiritual development will be something of lasting value, and this gives us a real purpose in life – to grow in Christ. The only thing a person takes with them into eternity is their character and this is being developed now as we produce the spiritual fruit of Christ-likeness.

Make Your Calling Sure

1:9 But concerning the one who lacks such things — he is blind. That is to say, he is nearsighted, since he has forgotten about the cleansing of his past sins.

It seems that Peter foresees a danger for those who do not heed his exhortation. Those who, having received the Lord Jesus Christ as Saviour, fail to go on and develop in their spiritual life, are blind. That is to say, they have no understanding of what God's purpose was in saving them from their sins. No one can stay where they are in the spiritual life. If you are not going forward, then you can only go back.

1:10–11 Therefore, brothers and sisters, make every effort to be sure of your calling and election. For by doing this you will never stumble into sin. For thus an entrance into the eternal kingdom of our Lord and Savior, Jesus Christ, will be richly provided for you.

Going on with Christ, and growing up into Him, is the only safeguard against the danger of such backsliding (Heb 2:1), for as we walk on the way heavenward, God will open the gates of the eternal kingdom wide to welcome us inside.

The Word of God

God's Word to be Remembered

1:12–13 Therefore, I intend to remind you constantly of these things even though you know them and are well established in the truth that you now have. Indeed, as long as I am in this tabernacle, I consider it right to stir you up by way of a reminder,

Peter realized the importance of Christians being diligent about maintaining their relationship with God. In keeping with Christ's final command to him, Peter was determined that, as long as he lived, he would not neglect his God-given duty to feed Christ's sheep and lambs (John 21:15–17). Peter had learned that constant exhortation and encouragement is necessary to help believers keep going, even for those who are already mature in faith.

1:14 since I know that my tabernacle will soon be removed, because our Lord Jesus Christ revealed this to me.

Peter knew he was approaching the time of his death. The Lord Jesus Christ had clearly foretold after his resurrection that Peter was to be executed (John 21:18–19). Tradition tells that he was crucified upside down; yet Peter sees this merely as laying aside his body, his temporary home (a tabernacle is a tent, not a permanent residence), so that he might enter his eternal home in heaven (2 Cor 5:1). All believers should have the same confidence as they approach death. For us, dying means stepping out of our earthly existence into eternal life with Christ. This joyful experience is the fulfilment of our earthly pilgrimage.

1:15 Indeed, I will also make every effort that, after my departure, you have a testimony of these things.

Peter wanted the church to have a permanent record of his teachings, just as he received them from the Lord Jesus Christ. That is why we have 1 and 2 Peter in our Bibles today.

The Fulfilment of God's Word Witnessed

1:16–18 For we did not follow cleverly concocted fables when we made known to you the power and return of our Lord Jesus Christ; no, we were eyewitnesses of his grandeur. For he received honor and glory from God the Father, when that voice was conveyed to him by the Majestic Glory: "This is my dear Son, in whom I am delighted." When this voice was conveyed from heaven, we ourselves heard it, for we were with him on the holy mountain.

What Peter wrote was so important that it had to be preserved for all generations. It is not a book of fables – stories deliberately written by men in order to teach moral lessons. Instead, it is the eyewitness account of one who had lived 3½ years with the Lord Jesus Christ, who saw his glory on the holy mountain and who later became a witness of his death and resurrection. Peter is referring to the time when he, James and John had seen the Lord transfigured before them, and a voice came from heaven to them which said, "This is my beloved Son, in whom I am well pleased" (Matt. 17:1–5). We know it's true, says Peter, we heard it, we were there!

God's Word Inspired

1:19 Moreover, we possess the prophetic word as an altogether reliable thing. You do well if you pay attention to this as you would to a light shining in a murky place, until the day dawns and the morning star rises in your hearts.

All that they had witnessed the Lord Jesus Christ do was in fulfillment of the prophetic Scriptures. Peter exhorts his readers to pay careful attention to the word of God. In this dark world of sin, it is the only light that will guide us to God and to heaven. If we follow it, will lead us all the way to where there is no darkness at all, but only the eternal light of God's presence. That is when we shall be forever with the Lord.

1:20–21 Above all, you do well if you recognize this: No prophecy of Scripture ever comes about by the prophet's own imagination, for no prophecy was ever borne of human impulse; rather, men carried along by the Holy Spirit spoke from God.

Peter gives his readers a basic lesson in Bible study. It is a lesson that Jesus Himself gave to his disciples (John 10:35). We believe that the Bible is the infallible word of God. God is the author of this book. Holy men of God were moved by the Holy Spirit and wrote down exactly what he told them to – even though they did not fully understand it (see 1 Peter 1:10–12). The Scripture cannot be understood merely by human skill, no matter how intellectually capable the interpreter. Only God, through the lens of his Son and the light of his Spirit, can give us the divinely intended interpretation (2 Tim 3:16).

Discussion Questions for Chapter 1

1. Why did Peter consider himself a servant of Jesus Christ?

2. What has God given us so that we might become more like Christ (v. 4)?

3. Why does Peter warn his readers (vv. 9–11) to make every effort to follow Christ and grow in God's grace?

4. In what way is God's word infallible?

Going Deeper – God's Infallible Word

In what sense is God's word infallible? And what is the Christian's relationship to that word? Let us look again at 2 Peter 1:19–21:

> Moreover, we possess the prophetic word as an altogether reliable thing. You do well if you pay attention to this as you would to a light shining in a murky place, until the day dawns and the morning star rises in your hearts. Above all, you do well if you recognize this: No prophecy of Scripture ever comes about by the prophet's own imagination, for no prophecy was ever borne of human impulse; rather, men carried along by the Holy Spirit spoke from God.

Firstly, we should notice that Peter's claim that, "men carried along by the Holy Spirit spoke from God," is the equivalent of Paul's statement in 1 Tim 3:16, "Every Scripture is inspired by God."

Peter lived before the time of printed Bibles, and before the multitudes of modern translations were available! But when we say Peter views the Scripture as infallible, that does not mean Peter would deny that an individual copy of the Bible might contain a typo, or that one word translated "steal" in the NET, for example, might be just as well translated "help himself" by the NIV (taken from John 12:6). Peter sees Scripture as infallible in the sense that it proceeds not from the mind or heart of a man or woman writing about God, but that it proceeds from the heart and mind of God, communicating and revealing the truth about himself to all people. The Scripture is a reliable record of who God is, for it is his own testimony – bearing in mind that Peter would regard God as a 100% reliable witness (cf. Numbers 23:19, "God is not a man, that he should lie;" Titus 1:2, "God, who does not lie" and Hebrews 6:18, "it is impossible for God to lie"). Consequently, since all Scripture is a true record, it follows that Scripture must agree with Scripture, and so Scripture is its own best interpreter. This means that whatever we learn of God in one passage of the Bible must be balanced against what we find in all other passages, for as Jesus himself taught his disciples, "the Scripture cannot be broken" (John 10:35).

Of course, when Peter speaks of Scripture, he initially[1] has in mind the Hebrew Scriptures, which Christians today might call the Old Testament. Peter had witnessed in Jesus the fulfillment of the prophetic Scriptures, which gave him even greater certainty of the reliability of God's word.

Not only so, but since Peter understood the believer's spiritual life was created through their faith in Christ, who is the fulfillment of God's word, he also recognized that the Scriptures were useful for promoting and producing godliness in the Christian life. This, perhaps, is the equivalent of Paul's view in 2 Tim 3:16–17 concerning the practical usefulness of Scripture:

> *Every Scripture is inspired by God and useful for teaching, for reproof, for correction, and for training in righteousness, that the person dedicated to God may be capable and equipped for every good work.*

As Peter exhorts the church to obey the word, he encourages them to allow the transforming power of the word to change their lives for the better. So, we find that Christians are never without a reliable guide in their lives, for God's word will always, infallibly, reveal God's will. It is, "a lamp to walk by, and a light to illumine my path" (Psalm 119:105).

---

[1] Interestingly, as we will deal with in more detail in later chapters, in 2 Peter 3:16, Peter appears to regard Paul's letters as Scripture, as he compares Paul's writings to "the rest of the Scriptures."

2 Peter 2

Themes in Chapter 2

The whole of chapter 2 is a warning against false prophets and the way they seek to lead the church away from Christ. Peter warns against accepting their teaching and adopting their practices. However, it is of note (despite the examples of false teaching given in the verse-by-verse section) that Peter does not expand on the content of their teaching. Instead he chooses to identify these people in terms of their immoral, debauched and hypocritical lifestyles.

No doubt Peter here is recalling the teaching of Jesus who said:

> Watch out for false prophets, who come to you in sheep's clothing but inwardly are voracious wolves. You will recognize them by their fruit. Grapes are not gathered from thorns or figs from thistles, are they? In the same way, every good tree bears good fruit, but the bad tree bears bad fruit. A good tree is not able to bear bad fruit, nor a bad tree to bear good fruit. Every tree that does not bear good fruit is cut down and thrown into the fire. So then, you will recognize them by their fruit. (Matthew 7:15–20)

Since Jesus declared that it would be by their fruit we would know them, Peter draws attention to the bitter fruit of sin in their lives. False teachers are dangerous for this reason, they lead God's people away from the truth, and lead them into sin which in turn brings them under divine judgment. In the Old Testament, idolatrous false prophets and corrupt leaders led the people of Israel to break the commands of God. This resulted in widespread backsliding and eventually God's intervening to judge his people as they were taken as exiles to a foreign country. The ultimate result of God's harsh but gracious action was the restoration of true worship in the hearts of the people, and their return to the homeland (Ezekiel 11:17–20; 37:12–14), even though it would only be through Christ that the ultimate fulfillment of this promise would come—a full reconciliation with God.

The rhetoric of Peter's argument is that the sinful way of life of the false teachers stands in contrast with the life of Christ, whose example we are to follow, however imperfectly. He highlights not only that

God's final and eternal judgment on these people will be severe, and that his displeasure will be evident long before then. In verse 3, he writes that this judgment, "is not asleep," meaning it will surely come in God's time.

The characteristic vices of the false prophets are clear for all to see: they live according to the unclean lusts of the flesh; they will not come under God-ordained authority, for they are self-willed, doing their own thing; they are like brute beasts inasmuch as they have no spiritual enlightenment, or of they do, they reject and refuse to live according to its implications; they are carousers, drunken party louts who are brazen, since they behave in this way in broad daylight, not just the night; they are adulterous (spiritually by unfaithfulness to God, and literally, defiling the institution of marriage); they have no self-restraint (they "cannot cease from sinning"); they are completely given over to greed, covetousness and the love of money; they promise so much but have nothing to give, they promise freedom but are bound by sin, they allure others to join them in abandoning the truth; and what is worse, they are not ignorant of the truth, but being fully aware of it, they do all they can to undermine it in their own lives and the lives of others.

This perhaps introduces the most tragic theme of all in this chapter, that of backsliding. False teachers in the Christian church generally emerge from those who have known the truth, and experienced its benefits, but who then reject and despise its power, authority, and blessing. Peter perhaps here has in mind the parable of the sower (Matt 13:1–23), where Jesus taught how different groups of people would react to the gospel message. In the explanation of that parable, Jesus taught how some would gladly receive his word and make a start on the Christian way, but when persecution came, or the love of material things overtook them, they would fall away. Yet Peter goes even further here, and may have in mind something worse. It is something he had encountered in Samaria (Acts 8:9–13, 18–24) where he met a man named Simon, a sorcerer who had at first been positively affected by the gospel, yet who sought to use this good news for his own ends. Peter rebuked him with a grave warning of eternal punishment, but Acts offers no further report on whether this rebuke succeeded in bringing Simon to true repentance. Acts later reports that false teachers were in the church (Acts 15:1; 20:29) and Jude's comment on these people is that they have "secretly slipped in among you" (Jude 1:4; see also Paul's view in Gal 2:4).

Peter's pastoral concern comes across strongly in this section, since his description of the false prophets, God's judgment on them, and their influence in the church is all aimed at keeping the believers focused on Christ and safeguarding them from backsliding (2 Pet 3:17).

In the church today, false teaching may or may not have aspects in common with first-century heresies, but the attitude and lifestyle of the ungodly remain characterized by sin, and a denial of the fact that Christ came to save us from our vices, not to encourage us to continue in them.

Verse-by-Verse

False Prophets

2:1 But false prophets arose among the people, just as there will be false teachers among you. These false teachers will infiltrate your midst with destructive heresies, even to the point of denying the Master who bought them. As a result, they will bring swift destruction on themselves.

In the last chapter we learned that the prophetic Scriptures were not composed by men, but by God's Holy Spirit. The Holy Spirit inspired holy men of God to speak or write down the words just as he taught them. In the days when God's prophets spoke, there were also false prophets among God's people. Similarly, in the New Testament age there are false teachers in God's church.

These false teachers have one aim – to deceive God's people and lead them away from Christ. They seek to destroy the good work God is doing in the lives of believers. They do this by attacking and undermining both the faith of individuals and the truth on which that faith is based (e.g. 2 Tim 2:17–18). Peter warns that the errors of these false teachers are very subtle. There are many kinds of false teachers today. Some will deceive others by their outrageous and clearly unscriptural teachings (e.g. Jehovah's Witnesses). Others, knowing that more experienced believers will not be taken in by such obvious errors, are more cunning. What they say may appear to be right, at least in part. It all sounds so plausible and we can be deceived into thinking that such teaching is not harmful.

Although the devil sometimes comes to us like a roaring lion, when he wants to deceive he comes disguised as an angel of light (2 Cor 11:13–14). False teachers will go so far as to "deny the Master (or Lord) who bought them." What does this mean? It means, firstly, that they will deny the truth of Christ's identity. Whether overtly or in more subtle ways they will deny that Christ is God "come in the flesh" (see 1 John 4:2–3). In addition, they will deny what Christ has done, both in personal terms (they will deny their own experience of his salvation), and also in more general terms (they will deny what Christ has accomplished by his death and resurrection). For example, there were teachers in Paul's day who taught that Gentile believers in Christ also had to be circumcised and keep the law in order to be saved (Acts 15:1). Paul refused to accept this teaching, because Christ had kept all the requirements of the law and had taken the penalty of the law in dying for everyone's sin, so that we might be saved by trusting in Christ. Peter affirms that swift destruction will come upon those who deny Christ's deity, or his humanity, or the full salvation he provides.

2:2 And many will follow their debauched lifestyles. Because of these false teachers, the way of truth will be slandered.

Peter warns that many (he means in the professing church) will follow the immoral and unrestrained way of life which the false teachers practice and promote. Their lifestyle will cause unbelievers to speak evil of the church and of Jesus Christ Himself. Their "debauched lifestyles" reveal that these false teachers mistake liberty for license. They assert that since they are saved by grace, no law applies to them and they may do as they please. Paul refutes such teaching in Rom 6:1–2. Christ does not tolerate immoral behavior in his church (e.g. Rev 2:20–23).

2:3 And in their greed they will exploit you with deceptive words. Their condemnation pronounced long ago is not sitting idly by; their destruction is not asleep.

These false teachers are motivated by greed and will attempt to make a financial gain from the church by cleverly deceiving it. That ministers should receive a financial reward for their ministry is acceptable and biblical (e.g. 1 Tim 5:17–18), but even so, financial gain should never be the motive of ministry (1 Pet 5:2; 1 Tim 6:1–10). False teachers strive to win followers, not for Christ, but for themselves (Acts 20:30) and reap substantial rewards for their deception. It will not be long before the righteous judgment of God falls upon them.

Judgment on False Teachers

In this section, Peter reminds his readers of God's holiness and of his judgment upon sin by quoting several examples from the Old Testament. We will notice that Peter does not spare his harsh language about false teachers; he clearly believes they should and will be most severely punished by God.

2:4 For if God did not spare the angels who sinned, but threw them into hell and locked them up in chains in utter darkness, to be kept until the judgment.

The angels who followed Lucifer in his rebellious attempt to seize the throne of God (see Isaiah 14:14 and Luke 10:18) were cast down and imprisoned in the darkness of hell, where they are to be kept until the day of judgment before being cast into the lake of fire.

2:5 And if he did not spare the ancient world, but did protect Noah, a herald of righteousness, along with seven others, when God brought a flood on an ungodly world,

Because of the violence and corruption of man in the days of Noah, God flooded the world and destroyed the wicked. Only those who believed God's word and accepted his way of salvation (the ark) were saved. They were Noah, his wife, his three sons and their wives (Gen 7:7).

2:6 and if he turned to ashes the cities of Sodom and Gomorrah when he condemned them to destruction, having appointed them to serve as an example to future generations of the ungodly,

Because of the evil practices of the people of Sodom and Gomorrah (the Old Testament describes both their sexual violence and homosexuality in these terms: Gen 13:13; 18:20; 19:4–5), God destroyed these cities and everyone in them with fire sent down from heaven (Gen 19:24). This action was intended to warn others of the final punishment of the wicked and of all those whose names are not found written in the Lamb's book of life (Jude 1:7; Rev 20:15). Phillips calls it, "a fearful example to those who wanted to live in defiance of his laws."

2:7–8 and if he rescued Lot, a righteous man in anguish over the debauched lifestyle of lawless men,(for while he lived among them day after day, that righteous man was tormented in his righteous soul by the lawless deeds he saw and heard)

The only people to be spared when God punished Sodom were Lot and his family, partly because Lot was a righteous man, and partly because Abraham had interceded on his behalf (Gen 18:16–33). Although he lived among the people, Lot did not consent to their actions but was appalled by what he heard and saw around him each day.

2:9 — if so, then the Lord knows how to rescue the godly from their trials, and to reserve the unrighteous for punishment at the day of judgment,

In view of these examples from Scripture, we can be assured that God will neither condemn the just, for he is the God of our salvation (1 Thess 5:9), nor acquit the wicked. He will see to it that the unrepentant do not escape his judgment (2 Thess 1:9).

2:10 especially those who indulge their fleshly desires and who despise authority. Brazen and insolent, they are not afraid to insult the glorious ones. This is especially true of those who follow the desires of their sinful nature and indulge in corrupt passions.

The seriousness of sexually immoral behavior lies in the fact that those who practice it despise of the moral order of the Creator. They despise all authority but especially God's authority – for in fact all authority is given by God (Rom 13:1). They are self-willed and self-loving, unwilling to submit to God. They are not afraid to make irreverent statements about God or other heavenly beings. They scoff about the glories of the unseen world, treating them as trivial or meaningless and are even prepared to make jokes about God, his word and the matters of his spiritual kingdom.

2:11 yet even angels, who are much more powerful, do not bring a slanderous judgment against them before the Lord.

Yet even the angels, who are superior in might and power to humans, do not bring insulting accusations about other angelic beings (including the devil) before the Lord. Angels realize that it is not their place to make judgments. Since it is God who has created all beings it is he alone who has the right to rebuke or pass judgment on them. This is why (as Jude tells us in Jude 1:9) Michael the archangel, when contesting with the devil about the body of Moses, did not dare insult him but came in the authority of the LORD God and said "The LORD rebuke you!"

2:12–13 But these men, like irrational animals — creatures of instinct, born to be caught and destroyed — do not understand whom they are insulting, and consequently in their destruction they will be destroyed, suffering harm as the wages for their harmful ways. By considering it a pleasure to carouse in broad daylight, they are stains and blemishes, indulging in their deceitful pleasures when they feast together with you.

Brute beasts ("irrational animals" in the NET, above) do not have human understanding. They are like cattle: bred and killed for food. Similarly, these false teachers have no understanding of spiritual things and speak evil of whatever they do not understand. Since they have not experienced spiritual reality they cannot understand it, and so think it must be nonsense and pour scorn on it. This is a serious matter, and they will receive terrible judgment for this – they will utterly perish in their sin (Rom 6:23). They enjoy indulging in shameless revelry and drunken parties in broad daylight – even in the fellowship of the church. This was possibly happening in the so-called "love feasts," a kind of church supper involving the communion which degenerated into an excuse for a party. The practice is condemned by Paul in 1 Cor 11:21–22. These people, says Peter, are unsightly pimples on the public face of the church. However, they are only deceiving themselves if they think that what they are doing will go unpunished.

2:14 Their eyes, full of adultery, never stop sinning; they entice unstable people. They have trained their hearts for greed, these cursed children!

Eyes being "full of adultery" could refer to that spiritual adultery which comes from being a friend of the world (James 4:4) and to the insatiable lust and craving for all that this world has to offer. Yet it could also be another reference to their immoral sexual behavior. They deliberately mislead others who are not yet firmly established in the faith so as to get something out of them. Phillips says, " Their technique of getting what they want is, through long practice, highly developed." They are under God's curse ("cursed children") and so will be forever condemned.

2:15–16 By forsaking the right path they have gone astray, because they followed the way of Balaam son of Bosor, who loved the wages of unrighteousness, yet was rebuked for his own transgression (a dumb donkey, speaking with a human voice, restrained the prophet's madness).

These people have forsaken what they know to be the right way – that is, the difficult path of being a disciple of Jesus (Matt 16:24). Instead they love self-indulgence and the easy life. Balaam, a heathen prophet, loved such a lifestyle. God clearly told him not to go with Israel's enemy Balak to place a curse on Israel. Yet the allure of money was too much for him and he went to do exactly what God had told him not to do. God intervened to prevent Balaam pronouncing the curse and even caused a donkey to speak with a human voice and rebuke the money-loving prophet (see Numbers 22).

2:17–18 These men are waterless springs and mists driven by a storm, for whom the utter depths of darkness have been reserved. For by speaking high-sounding but empty words they are able to entice, with fleshly desires and with debauchery, people who have just escaped from those who reside in error.

False teachers are wells without water for they promise a lot but have nothing to offer. The saying, "Empty vessels make the most noise," applies to these people who make loud foolish boasts but have nothing to give. Peter similarly compares them to clouds blown along by the wind without giving rain, for they are empty. They are good for nothing – apostates – unprofitable servants who will be cast into outer darkness. No doubt here Peter recalls Christ's teaching from Matt 5:13 and 25:30 (see also John 15:6. and Heb 6:7–8).

Many, who perhaps have been partly awakened to their need of God, will be taken in by their lies. Many people would like religion without restraint, a faith that promises heaven to those who sin and a license for everyone to do whatever they want. It all sounds very appealing to them because of the lusts of their hearts, and so they are prepared to believe the lie.

2:19 Although these false teachers promise such people freedom, they themselves are enslaved to immorality. For whatever a person succumbs to, to that he is enslaved.

When these teachers proclaim "liberty," they are actually encouraging "slavery." Peter is once again thinking of the words of the Lord Jesus Christ when he says that this "liberty" is nothing more than bondage, for a person who sins becomes a slave to whatever has overcome and mastered them (see John 8:34. Also read Rom 6:16–18).

2:20–22 For if after they have escaped the filthy things of the world through the rich knowledge of our Lord and Savior Jesus Christ, they again get entangled in them and succumb to them, their last state has become worse for them than their first. For it would have been better for them never to have known the way of righteousness than, having known it, to turn back from the holy commandment that had been delivered to them. They are illustrations of this true proverb: "A dog returns to its own vomit," and "A sow, after washing herself, wallows in the mire."

Peter ends this chapter with a warning that is repeated in various ways throughout the New Testament (e.g. Heb 6:4–8 and Heb 10:26–31; Jas 5:19–20). Anyone who has received the Lord Jesus Christ as Saviour and has been delivered from the power of sin yet turns back and is entangled again with the old life of sin, is worse off afterward than when they started. After all, their previous life of sin was lived in ignorance. They have afterward returned to their old way of life despite knowing what they should do. This only serves to increase their responsibility and guilt before God.

The terrible fact is that it would have been better for them to have perished in their sin and ignorance than to have known the way of righteousness and then afterward reject it and forsake it.

It is an observable fact that dogs will sometimes lick up their own vomit after being sick. Similarly, backsliders have chosen to take up their life of sin again instead of continuing to follow Christ. The washed pig returns to the mud, and sadly there are those who have been washed in the blood of Christ but have chosen to return to a life of sin.

Discussion Questions for Chapter 2

1. In what ways might false teachers, "deny the Master who bought them?"

2. Discuss some of the sinful characteristics of false teachers – the fruit by which they may be recognized. Be wary of these vices in your own life too!

3. Why do you think that Peter says, "it would have been better for them never to have known the way of righteousness" (v. 21)?

4. In what ways should Peter's warning about false teachers affect the way you live your Christian life?

Going Deeper – Once Saved Always Saved?

Is it correct to say, "Once saved always saved?" What a subject to get into in a small book like this! Yet it is a question which comes up again and again in study groups everywhere. Perhaps this itself indicates that it is a question that has been inadequately answered, or that the answers often given have failed to convince the church at large. However, as I attempt to answer the question here, I must begin by admitting it is by no means a straightforward one. There is the need for the answer to this question to be balanced, keeping the tension between the seemingly contradictory statements of the New Testament on this subject.

On the one hand, the New Testament is full of assurance for those who have put their trust in Christ and his salvation. A few well-known verses will suffice to illustrate:

> I give them eternal life, and they will never perish; no one will snatch them from my hand. (John 10:28)

> For I am convinced that neither death, nor life, nor angels, nor heavenly rulers, nor things that are present, nor things to come, nor powers, nor height, nor depth, nor anything else in creation will be able to separate us from the love of God in Christ Jesus our Lord. (Rom 8:38–39)

> "I will never leave you and I will never abandon you." (Heb 13:5)

Clearly, to those with noble and good hearts, who are sincerely trusting Christ as Savior, God wants to impart assurance of everlasting life, a life which will never be taken away from us or lost by us.

Yet herein lies an apparent difficulty. For the same infallible, divinely inspired Scriptures which offer believers assurance, also warn believers of the dangers of falling away. Again, let's look at one or two well-known examples:

> Therefore, dear friends, since you have been forewarned, be on your guard that you do not get led astray by the error of these unprincipled men and fall from your firm grasp on the truth. (2 Pet 3:17)

> If anyone does not remain in me, he is thrown out like a branch, and dries up; and such branches are gathered up and thrown into the fire, and are burned up. (John 15:6)

> See to it, brothers and sisters, that none of you has an evil, unbelieving heart that forsakes the living God. But exhort one another each day, as long as it is called "Today," that none of you may become hardened by sin's deception. For we have become partners with Christ, if in fact we hold our initial confidence firm until the end. As it says, *"Oh, that today you would listen as he speaks! Do not harden your hearts as in the rebellion."* (Heb 3:12–15)

> For it is impossible in the case of those who have once been enlightened, tasted the heavenly gift, become partakers of the Holy Spirit, tasted the good word of God and the miracles of the coming age, and then have committed apostasy, to renew them again to repentance, since they are crucifying the Son of God for themselves all over again and holding him up to contempt. For the ground that has soaked up the rain that frequently falls on it and yields useful vegetation for those who tend it receives a blessing from God. But if it produces thorns and thistles, it is useless and about to be cursed; its fate is to be burned. (Heb 6:4–8)

It occurs to me that the best way to receive any word from God is with an open heart. If our hearts are true to Christ, we will heed his warning. If our hearts are true to Christ, we will also accept the equally great assurance God gives to those who are his. From a biblical perspective, I can see no disparity between the righteous rejoicing in God's assurance, whilst at the same time being tender-hearted towards the warnings of God. Both are vital elements of the righteous soul's response to God.

To put this in more familiar, perhaps old-fashioned terms, this means that the perseverance of the saints (in terms of their abiding faithful to Christ) is necessary, but that it is also guaranteed for those who are called and kept by his grace. Yet to adopt the one view without grasping the other is to be unbalanced and deficient in our Christian experience. There is a balance here. If you are not concerned about the danger of falling away, then I would fear that you are actually falling away from the wholesome fear of the Lord, but if you are aware of the dangers, and tremble in your heart at the loving severity of God, then you may drink deeply of his eternal assurance, for you are certainly guarded by almighty power. Both God's assurance and his warnings are evidence of his infinite determination to keep and safeguard his people. What they *do not* give is any evidence that God's action will be positive to certain "chosen" people regardless of their response to his grace.

Thus, as we discussed in our study of 1 Peter, we accept that salvation is a sovereign act of God, but that this action does not preclude the idea of human responsibility. And if anyone disagrees with us, we would be gracious enough to admit, as Paul did, our own dimness of sight concerning such mysteries, and therefore accept that one must disagree with good grace!

> Oh, the depth of the riches and wisdom and knowledge of God! How unsearchable are his judgments and how fathomless his ways! (Rom 11:33)

1 Peter 3

Themes in Chapter 3

In chapter 3, Peter reveals his confidence in the words of God and of Christ and highlights the importance of remembering and taking them to heart. Indeed, verse 2 seems to suggest equivalence of the apostolic tradition with the words of the Old Testament prophets, as does verse 15.

Peter argues against scoffers who believe that God's judgment will not come (v. 3), by referring them to times in history when God acted suddenly to silence dissent, citing the example of Noah (vv. 5–7). He similarly argues against those who reject the assertion that Christ will come again (v. 4). The Christian hope of Jesus' return has not been delayed; it will occur (as Jesus said in Matt 25:13) at a time known only to God. This is something which he has not chosen to reveal to men. God is outside of time, and so even 1,000 years is like a day to him (note that Christians at this point had waited less than 100 years for the return of Jesus). Moreover, God is patient, and the other side of the Noah story remains true also – that God holds his judgment back only so that others may repent and be saved.

In contrast to the views of some recent theologians, who speak only of the renewal of the present earth at Christ's coming, Peter's description of the end of the material universe indicates something beyond this (vv. 8–10). Peter, who argues for a personal and literal return of Jesus, argues equally for the literal creation of a new heaven and earth (v. 13).

In the light of these teachings, Peter calls his readers to live holy lives that please God (vv. 11, 14), and to avoid following the debauched lifestyles of false prophets, who distort God's word in order to draw followers away from Christ and to themselves. Peter comments on Paul's recent letters to the churches too, that these should be taken seriously, and in context it may be that Peter has in mind that the exhortations to holy living which Paul so frequently gave (e.g. 1 Thess 4:7) should be heeded and obeyed.

Instead, the believers should make every effort (as he had previously discussed in more detail chapter 1) to grow to know Jesus Christ and experience his grace in their lives. As they do, their devotion will be evident by their Christ-like behavior.

Verse-by-Verse

Godly Reminders

3:1 Dear friends, this is already the second letter I have written you, in which I am trying to stir up your pure mind by way of reminder:

Peter had written this and his previous letter so that the church would always have a record of his teaching, as it was handed down to him by Christ; and that by being reminded of his word, God's people might be stirred to obedience, service, worship and patience. All that is needed for our Christian life is provided for by the constant repetition and teaching of the Scriptures, and this is the responsibility of every minister of God's word (2 Tim 3:16–17; Acts 20:32). As believers, our minds (hearts, consciences) have been made pure by the cleansing of Jesus' blood (Heb 10.22) and by the action of the new birth (Tit 3.5), which accompanies our acceptance of the gospel message.

3:2 I want you to recall both the predictions foretold by the holy prophets and the commandment of the Lord and Savior through your apostles.

Since faith came to us by hearing God's word, Peter urges us to keep in mind what we have been taught. The message was foretold by the Old Testament prophets and was made clear by the Lord Jesus Christ, who entrusted the apostles to preach it to the people. Giving heed to Christ's teaching will guard us against error, wrong living, apathy, and indifference.

Scoffers

3:3–6 Above all, understand this: In the last days blatant scoffers will come, being propelled by their own evil urges and saying, "Where is his promised return? For ever since our ancestors died, all things have continued as they were from the beginning of creation." For they deliberately suppress this fact, that by the word of God heavens existed long ago and an earth was formed out of water and by means of water. Through these things the world existing at that time was destroyed when it was deluged with water.

In the last days (for Peter, this means as the time of Christ's coming draws near) many people will mock God's word and pour scorn on the gospel message. It is so today. In our country there are those who will do anything they can to undermine the gospel message or to prevent it from being heard. Such people, says J. B. Phillips, have only one guide in life – what they want for themselves. They hear the truth about the Lord Jesus Christ but mock it as if it were the very worst of fairy stories. Especially is this true of his coming again. They say, "Where is he then? If he was going to come again, he would surely have come by now, so he isn't coming at all." In fact, they are those who say that nothing in the Bible is true.

According to these people, nothing has changed from the beginning of creation. This does not mean they believe that God made the world (they do not), but rather that the universe runs itself without him. They do not believe in the resurrection, either, and they say that God will not judge the world. They want to believe this because they want to forget God and go their own way. They do not want the restraint that responsibility to a Creator God brings. They wish to cast off the restraints and restrictions of God's laws. In the words of the psalm, they say, "Let's tear off the shackles they've put on us! Let's free ourselves from their ropes!" (Ps 2:3). They say, "We are our own masters. We own our lips..." (Ps 12:4).

They deliberately forget that God has often intervened in human history. Peter makes reference to the most notable Old Testament example, the flood which, because of man's sin, destroyed the world in the days of Noah. Today, as we encounter such opposition to our Christian faith, the reality of God's intervention in the past points forward to his intervention in the future, and assures us that ultimately, everyone will know that our God reigns!

The End of this Age and the Eternal Ages to Come

3:7–10 But by the same word the present heavens and earth have been reserved for fire, by being kept for the day of judgment and destruction of the ungodly. Now, dear friends, do not let this one thing escape your notice, that a single day is like a thousand years with the Lord and a thousand years are like a single day. The Lord is not slow concerning his promise, as some regard slowness, but is being patient toward you, because he does not wish for any to perish but for all to come to repentance. But the day of the Lord will come like a thief; when it comes, the heavens will disappear with a horrific noise, and the celestial bodies will melt away in a blaze, and the earth and every deed done on it will be laid bare.

This present world will continue until the time ordained by God when he will judge its inhabitants. At that time the heavens and the earth will be destroyed by fire. Peter does not here elaborate on the nature or cause of this "fire," but there are certain points we can surmise from the following verses.

As Christians we should know that God's word is true. Although human beings live in the realm that is governed by time, he lives outside this constraint. It appears to men that he has delayed his coming, but he has not. What are 2000 years to him? He is eternal (Ps 90:2). He has fixed the day of Christ's coming again (Acts 17).

It is God's long-suffering that leads Him to give enough opportunity for everyone to hear the gospel and to repent. In the days of Noah, God waited 120 years for the same reason. However, the flood came at his appointed time and not a second later. It is not God's will that any should perish (see 2 Peter 3:9 and Tit 2:4), so no blame will ever be laid at God's door when some do; it will be their own fault. When the very last person who is going to be saved has been gathered in, then Christ will come. The timing of this event, as we have said, is fixed and determined by God, and known only to God Him. For us it will come suddenly and unexpectedly, just like when a thief breaks in, unannounced.

On that "Day of the Lord" the very elements – that is, all created things – will pass away (i.e. will cease to be). This is confirmed in Heb 12:26–27. The material universe is described as temporal (2 Cor 4:18), which means that it will pass away (1 Cor 7:31 and Ps 102:25–26). Isaiah 34:4 uses imagery of a scroll rolling up or leaves falling of a tree (see also Isa 51:6). I believe that when God removes his word of command which upholds creation then it will instantly cease to exist, just as instantly as it came into being when he spoke his word in Genesis 1. This will cause a tremendous generation of heat, rather like what is produced during nuclear fusion. However, this does not mean that it will be fusion which will cause the heat, for heat itself will cease to be.

Peter refers to a long period of time in this one verse, for we must distinguish between Christ's coming for his own, his coming to earth to reign and the final judgment. Briefly, we know that Christ will live and reign on this earth for 1000 years at his coming (millennium). It will be at the end of this period that the present earth and heavens will cease to exist, and the wicked will be judged (Rev 20:11–15). Once the wicked have been banished forever, God will make a new heaven and new earth (Rev 21).

3:11–13 Since all these things are to melt away in this manner, what sort of people must we be, conducting our lives in holiness and godliness, while waiting for and hastening the coming of the day of God? Because of this day, the heavens will be burned up and dissolve, and the celestial bodies will melt away in a blaze! But, according to his promise, we are waiting for new heavens and a new earth, in which righteousness truly resides.

Since this world is passing away, we should always be living for the next, according to the values of the world to come (holiness, godliness, love etc.) while we wait and eagerly anticipate the day when Christ shall come, who shall change our bodies and deliver us forever from the presence of sin. Peter has already told us that sin distresses the child of God (2 Pet 2:7–8), and in the new heaven and earth, by virtue of Christ's death, there will be no sin but only righteousness forever. We will be with the Lord forevermore (Rev 22:3–5 and Rev 21:3–5) in a blessed state will never end (Isa 66:22).

Continuing Steadfastly in the Faith

3:14 Therefore, dear friends, since you are waiting for these things, strive to be found at peace, without spot or blemish, when you come into his presence.

Since this is our hope, we should be careful not to be at variance with God or with one another (1 Thess 5:13). Instead we should live blameless lives before him (Phil 2:15). Because of all that Christ has done for us, we should want to please him. As God's people, if we sin, we are to confess our sins, and he will forgive us (1 John 1:9). If we are unrepentant about our sin, we will be chastened so that we might not be condemned with the world (1 Cor 11:32).

3:15–16 And regard the patience of our Lord as salvation, just as also our dear brother Paul wrote to you, according to the wisdom given to him, speaking of these things in all his letters. Some things in these letters are hard to understand, things the ignorant and unstable twist to their own destruction, as they also do to the rest of the Scriptures.

Peter wants Christians to know that when we do wrong, God does not cast us off, but disciplines us as a Father his child, so that we might share in his holiness (Heb 12:6–10). His love remains constant to us and the fact that he chooses to deal with us in this way shows that he is long-suffering (i.e. is prepared, in love, to put up with a lot). It is this loving patience of God which accounts for the fact that, having been saved, we are kept by his power.

Peter recognizes that Paul, who had also written to the church, had been given wisdom and understanding by God through the revelations which he had received (Gal 1:12; Eph 3:3). As a beloved brother, he had written along similar lines to the church previously about the long-suffering of the Lord. Peter recognizes Paul's writings as being *Scripture* and that some of what he says is difficult to understand. Those who are untaught in the word of God and who are not established firmly in the faith distort his teachings to fit themselves. They try to make them mean what they are not intended to mean, and they also do this to the rest of the Scriptures, thereby bringing about their destruction. God will deal severely with all those who misrepresent and twist his word (Rev 22:18–19).

3:17–18 Therefore, dear friends, since you have been forewarned, be on your guard that you do not get led astray by the error of these unprincipled men and fall from your firm grasp on the truth. But grow in the grace and knowledge of our Lord and Savior Jesus Christ. To him be the honor both now and on that eternal day.

Since we have been instructed in the truth, we have a great responsibility to remain alert and watchful unless we are also carried along with others who turn from the truth and so fall from our present steadfast faith in Christ. If we continue to love, learn and live the truth, then instead of being led astray, we will continue to grow in the grace and knowledge of our Lord and Saviour Jesus Christ – getting to know him and his perfect will for our lives as it unfolds in our walk with Him. We join Peter with the heartfelt praise: to him (the Lord Jesus Christ) be glory both now and throughout all eternity. Amen.

Discussion Questions for Chapter 3

1. Discuss the ways in which the apparent delay in Christ's return is not actually a delay at all from God's viewpoint.

2. What warnings does Peter give for those who scoff and deny God's involvement in the present world?

3. In what way does the "patience of our Lord," account for our salvation?

4. What do you think it means for believers to, "grow in the grace and knowledge of our Lord and Savior Jesus Christ?"

Going Deeper – Paul's Letters as Scripture

We read in chapter 3 a hint that Peter somehow equated Paul's letters with the rest of Scripture. Is there really any evidence that Paul himself regarded them in this way?

Paul's repeated claim throughout his letters is that he was an apostle sent by Jesus Christ (e.g. 1 Cor 1:1; Gal 1:1; 1 Tim 1:1) and entrusted with God's message (Gal 2:7; 1 Tim 1:11). He insists that he is equal to all the other apostles, including Peter, who had been directly taught and commissioned by Christ (1 Cor 15:7–10; 2 Cor 12:11). This message was of course the good news about Jesus, which he claimed to have received in a manner equivalent to that by which the prophets received their message – not from any man but by direct revelation from God (Gal 1:11–12; this perhaps is not a reference to basic Christian teaching, which he may have encountered in the days when he persecuted the church, so much as to his inspired understanding of its full implications). It is also clear that Paul saw himself as being entrusted with the task of delivering this message to God's people.

Having said that, Paul's letters to the churches were precisely that – letters. Some contain more doctrine than others, and there are occasions when Paul uses up the page to send polite personal greetings, or to offer what he sees as an opinion (e.g. 1 Cor 7:12). Elsewhere he seems to be quoting sayings, or even hymns, current among the believers.

Even so, without a doubt Paul claimed to have both authority and inspiration from God to teach the truths of the Christian faith (1 Tim 1:11; 2:7; Col 1:25). This seems to be on the one hand, a claim of the equivalence of his ministry to that of the Old Testament prophets, and on the other hand, it follows the traditions of the rabbis in expounding sacred text.

So, although it is not clear that Paul regarded his own letters as sacred Scripture, it does appear that he regarded the truths which he expounded within them to be sacred, inspired by the Holy Spirit, and on a par with anything contained in the Scriptures. Indeed, he sees that the revelation he has been given is based on the law and the prophets, and that it was hidden therein until the insight which Christ gave to his apostles meant it could be made known to all believers (Eph 3:4–5).

Paul certainly intended his readers to take his letters as authoritative. It is not impossible that he might have anticipated their later being grouped together, rather like the teachings of the rabbis, as a collection of sacred writings. Indeed, collections even of the Greek philosophers were common in Paul's time. It would probably be a step too far, however, for us to suggest that Paul foresaw the creation of anything like our New Testament, let alone if he expected his letters to be included in it. Instead, his intention may have been more like Peter's, that that the church might have a permanent record of Christian doctrine:

> Indeed, I will also make every effort that, after my departure, you have a testimony of these things. (2 Pet 1:15)

.

Sample Answers to Discussion Questions

These answers are not necessarily the only "correct" answers to the questions given but are intended to help and guide you in your study.

Chapter 1

1. Jesus was Peter's Lord. Peter was carrying out his ministry to the church for Christ's sake, and in obedience to Christ's command; it was not his own idea.

2. God has given us the promises of his word so that by faith and obedience we might become more like Jesus who always obeyed his Father.

3. Peter believed that effort – in cooperation with God – was an important factor in spiritual growth, which prevents backsliding.

4. Although Bible translations may differ on minor points, the Bible is infallible since it is a revelation given by God about himself – it is not second-hand knowledge.

Chapter 2

1. False teachers deny the Master by denying Christ's deity or contradicting his teaching. Also, their disobedience to his commands reveals that they have disowned his Lordship.

2. Lust, self-will, rejecting spiritual enlightenment of God's word, drunken, adulterers, no self-restraint, greedy, covetous, love money, undermining truth in the lives of others.

3. I think those who are ignorant of truth are less guilty than those who know it and yet reject it. They will be punished more severely.

4. Peter's warning is not only that I should be careful to follow true teaching, but also that I should avoid the corrupt lifestyle modeled by the false teachers.

Chapter 3

1. For two reasons: i) God is outside time, so 1,000 years is no time at all to him; ii) God is patient, giving plenty of time and opportunity for everyone to repent and be saved.

2. Peter warns that God's judgment was revealed suddenly and unexpectedly against scoffers in the past, and that it shall be again in the future.

3. God will not give up on us just because we fail. He warns us away from failure and restores us when we repent, all as part of his plan of safeguarding us in Christ.

4. As we get to know Jesus more through the revelation of his Spirit and the word of God, we are transformed to become more like him. As we live in obedience to his teaching, our lives will reflect his.

Bibliography

1.   *The Amplified New Testament*. Michigan: Zondervan, 1987.

2.   Vine, W. E. *Expository Dictionary of New Testament Words*. London: Marshall, Morgan & Scott, 1940.

3.   Ellicott, Charles John. *Ellicott's Bible Commentary In One Volume*. London: Pickering & Inglis Ltd, 1971.

4.   *The Living Bible*. Tyndale, 1974.

5.   *Matthew Henry Complete Commentary*. London: Marshall, Morgan & Scott, 1960.

6.   Moo, Douglas, *2 Peter, Jude: From Biblical Text — to Contemporary Life* (The NIV Application Commentary). Grand Rapids: Zondervan, 1996.

7.   Gene L. Green, *Jude and 2 Peter*. Grand Rapids: Baker, 2008.

Appendix – How to Use this Study Guide

Good Bible study takes time. Set aside sufficient time to study the chapter on your own—or divide the chapter into two parts. Allow an hour if possible or at least half an hour for your study.

We recommend that you photocopy the discussion questions (or print them from www.biblestudiesonline.org.uk). Use one for yourself and distribute one each to every member of your study group. Having studied the verses on your own, arrange a meeting so you can join together and compare notes.

Always pray before you begin your study, that God will give you understanding. Then read the chapter itself, from whichever Bible version you prefer. Then sit down, in a quiet place, and read through each verse again together with the guide notes, taking time to reflect and think upon what you read. Make your own notes if possible; recording what God is showing you through the chapter, which might be somewhat different to the guide notes, especially if something is speaking to you personally from a certain verse or chapter. Be sure to share these insights later with your Bible study group. Again, close your study time with a short prayer. Remember that God himself is your greatest teacher, so you need to spend time with him if you wish to understand his word.

We recommend that you concentrate on no more than one chapter at a time. Reading the verses through again will help to ensure that what you have learned will stay in your heart and become part of your life.

Remember—God's word is not an academic textbook to be learned by rote. It is a living word to be hidden in your heart and obeyed in your life. May God bless you as you seek to follow him, employing the best method for spiritual growth which has ever been known to humankind—Bible study!

www.ingramcontent.com/pod-product-compliance
Lightning Source LLC
Chambersburg PA
CBHW072040060426
42449CB00010BA/2363